To Love This Life

$\mathcal{T}$he best and most beautiful things in the world cannot be seen nor even touched, but just felt in the heart.

To Love This Life

—— ∞ ——

Quotations by Helen Keller

SCHOLASTIC INC.

New York   Toronto   London   Auckland   Sydney
Mexico City   New Delhi   Hong Kong   Buenos Aires

ISBN 0-439-31913-7

12 11 10 9 8 7 6 5 4 3 2 1   1 2 3 4 5 6/0

Printed in the U.S.A.   40

First Scholastic printing, September 2001

Quotations in this volume are rendered with the original spellings.

Editor	Ellen Bilofsky
Librarian	Amy Boardley Watson
Cover design	Suzanne Lynch
Interior design	Holly Reid McLaughlin
Editor in chief	Natalie Hilzen

Contents

Foreword

Helen Keller was a woman of modesty, because despite her remarkable accomplishments she did not view herself as remarkable. Through her struggles to overcome the astounding odds against her she became famous; but her mission was to use the platform this gave her in the service of others. Without sight, she saw clearly into the souls of her fellow men and women, and without hearing she heard plainly the cries of people who suffered from poverty, from war, from disabilities, from discrimination.

Although she is often remembered for her handicaps, those who read her words inscribed in these pages will know her first as a great humanitarian—a peacemaker. Far from being relics of some misty past, her thoughts are beacons of plain truth for those of us who today still strive to attain the goals she set: a society where every individual, regardless of circumstance of birth and status, has the opportunity to achieve; an end to needless suffering; and peace throughout the world.

As someone whose primary obstacles in life were impediments to communicating with others, she dedicated herself to communication. Just as she was committed to her own independence, she was committed to fostering the independence of others. The joy with which she embraced life is evident in the sharpness and beauty of her observations, her sly wit, and her impatience with pretense.

This volume is testimony to the many facets of Helen Keller, but most of all to the legacy of her life. Her abiding concern was to leave the world a better place than she found it, and simply by leaving us her example, she succeeded admirably in that goal.

JIMMY CARTER

Former President Jimmy Carter is the founder and chairman of the Carter Center, an organization dedicated to preventing and resolving conflicts, enhancing freedom and democracy, and improving health. Through its River Blindness and Trachoma Programs, the Carter Center is part of a worldwide coalition fighting river blindness.

Preface

Winston Churchill called her "the greatest woman of the twentieth century." Mark Twain went even further, calling her "the most extraordinary product of all the ages."

Helen Keller was born in Tuscumbia, Alabama, on June 27, 1880. At the age of 18 months she was stricken with a sudden illness that would leave her both blind and deaf for the rest of her life. Up to this time, the little girl had shown a quick mind and a real joy for life that only the very young can know. Now she was in a dark and silent world that could not be penetrated.

After five years of this darkness and silence, Helen's mother discovered that there were places that might help the deaf and blind. It was Alexander Graham Bell, the famous inventor and teacher of deaf people, who put the family in touch with Michael Anagnos, the director of the Perkins Institution for the Blind in Boston; and he arranged for his star pupil, Anne Sullivan, to arrive in Tuscumbia on that fateful day in March 1887, to become Helen's Teacher.

With determination and compassion, Anne Sullivan literally took young Helen by the hand and led her into life. By pressing the letters of the manual alphabet into her hand, Anne would spell out the word for each object Helen touched. At first, word associations were difficult; but one day Annie spelled W-A-T-E-R into one of Helen's hands while the other felt the cold wetness, and Helen learned her first word.

I always knew I had a special connection to Helen Keller. I was born in Helen Keller Memorial Hospital and named after my great-great-aunt. I remember blindfolding myself with one of my mother's scarves and putting cotton balls in my ears to help me imagine what kind of world she must have lived in. After reading Helen Keller's autobiography, *The Story of My Life,* when I was 9 years old, I realized that Helen Keller did much more than learn what W-A-T-E-R stood for. I was amazed to learn that a deaf-blind person could learn to read, write, and speak in several languages. She would meet 10 United States presidents, receive the Presidential Medal of Freedom, and the rich and famous would call her their friend. But it was the moment I realized that Helen Keller's life was about helping others that I knew I would someday follow in her footsteps. Today, as Ambassador for the American Foundation for the Blind, I am fulfilling that dream. In this capacity—the same position held by my great-great-aunt—I share the message that Helen Keller's life was not just about being deaf and blind. It was about overcoming incredible odds, sacrificing for what you really want in life, and leaving the world better than you found it.

With the help of braille and a typewriter, this remarkable woman expressed her feelings, observations, and opinions to a world that was fascinated by her achievements. But her writings were only a part of her unique career. She never lost sight of the needs of her fellows who were blind and deaf-blind. From 1924 until her death, she was a member of the staff of the American Foundation for the Blind, serving as a counselor on national and international relations. She toured the United States, lecturing, visiting, talking, and praying for those who were blind, deaf, deaf-blind, or had some other disability.

In 1946, she began globe-circling tours with her companion Polly Thomson. During seven trips between 1946 and 1957 she visited 35 countries on five continents, and began a 40,000-mile tour of Asia when she was 75. Wherever she traveled, she brought hope and courage to millions.

So powerful a symbol of triumph did she become that she has an indisputable place in the history of our time and of times to come. Upon her death in 1968, just short of her 88th birthday, Senator Lister Hill of Alabama expressed the feelings of the world at the funeral services at the National Cathedral in Washington, D.C., when he said, "She will live on as one of the few, the immortal names not born to die. Her spirit will endure as long as man can read, and stories can be told of the woman who showed the world that there are no boundaries to courage and faith."

Her writings are presented here, at the sunset of one century and the dawning of another. They serve to illuminate her own being and to help others see themselves. They reveal this woman's great courage, and express the deep faith that is a main source of her strength. It is my hope that Helen Keller's words will touch you in ways you cannot even imagine. May they give you faith, courage, strength, and hope as we move into a new century.

KELLER JOHNSON-THOMPSON

Keller Johnson-Thompson is Ambassador for the American Foundation for the Blind in New York City.

Chronology

June 27, 1880

Helen Keller is born to Captain Arthur Henley Keller and Kate Adams Keller at Ivy Green in Tuscumbia, Alabama.

February 1882

After being struck by illness, Helen loses both her sight and hearing. No definitive diagnosis of the disease is ever determined.

Summer 1886

The Keller family meets with Dr. Alexander Graham Bell, who recommends contacting Michael Anagnos, director of Perkins Institution for the Blind in Boston. Captain Keller writes to Anagnos, requesting a teacher for Helen. Anagnos contacts his star pupil and valedictorian, Anne Mansfield Sullivan.

March 3, 1887

Anne Sullivan arrives in Tuscumbia and begins teaching Helen manual sign language.

April 5, 1887

Anne makes the "miracle" breakthrough, teaching Helen that "everything has a name," by spelling W-A-T-E-R into Helen's hand as water from the family's water pump flows over their hands.

May 1888

Anne, Helen, and Kate Keller travel north, visiting Alexander Graham Bell, and meeting President Grover

Cleveland at the White House, and visiting Anagnos at Perkins Institution.

Fall 1889

Anne and Helen return to Perkins, where Helen is considered a "guest" of the school.

November 1891

Helen sends Anagnos the story "The Frost King" as a birthday present. She is accused of plagiarism. By 1894, Anagnos had broken off his relationship with Helen and Anne.

October 1894

Helen and Anne travel to New York City, where Helen attends the Wright-Humason School for the Deaf.

August 19, 1896

Helen's father, Captain Keller, dies.

Fall 1896

Helen becomes a devout Swedenborgian.

October 1896

Helen is accepted as a pupil at the Cambridge School for Young Ladies, in preparation for attendance at Harvard's annex for women, Radcliffe College.

December 1897

Helen and Anne leave the Cambridge School and move to Wrentham, Massachusetts. Helen continues her college preparatory studies with the assistance of private tutors.

July 4, 1899

Helen receives her certificate of admission to Radcliffe College.

September 1900
Helen becomes a member of the freshman class of 1904 at Radcliffe.

March 1903
With the help of editor John Albert Macy, Helen writes *The Story of My Life*.

Spring 1904
Helen and Anne buy a home on seven acres of land in Wrentham.

June 28, 1904
Helen becomes the first deaf-blind individual to receive a bachelor of arts degree, graduating cum laude from Radcliffe.

May 3, 1905
Anne marries John Macy at Wrentham.

July 1908
Helen writes and publishes *The World I Live In*.

Spring, 1909
Helen and John Macy join the Socialist Party of Massachusetts, and Helen becomes a suffragist.

January 1913
Helen and Anne begin their career on the lecture circuit, which is to last more than 50 years. Helen writes and publishes *Out of the Dark*, a collection of socialist writings.

1914
John Macy leaves Anne, though they never officially divorce.

October 1914
Polly Thomson joins Helen and Anne's household.

November 1916

Peter Fagan, John Macy's assistant, proposes to Helen,
and they take out a marriage license in Boston.
Helen's mother forces her to publicly renounce her
engagement. Helen is sent to Montgomery, Alabama, to
visit family, while Anne and Polly travel to Lake Placid
and Puerto Rico in hopes of aiding Anne's failing health.

October 1917

Helen and Anne sell their farm in Wrentham and move
with Polly to Forest Hills, New York.

May 1918

Deliverance, a silent film based on Helen's life, is produced.

February 1920

Helen and Anne begin their vaudeville career, speaking
and answering questions on stage.

June 1921

Helen's mother, Kate Keller, dies.

October 1924

Helen and Anne begin their work with the American
Foundation for the Blind.

June 1925

Helen makes an appeal to the International Convention
of Lions Clubs, asking the Lions to become "Knights of
the Blind."

October 1927

My Religion, Helen's account of her Swedenborgian beliefs,
is published.

Spring 1929
Midstream, an autobiographical account of Helen's later life, is published.

April 1930
Helen, Anne, and Polly travel abroad for the first time, visiting Scotland, Ireland, and England for over six months.

April 1931
Helen, Anne, and Polly participate in the first World Council for the Blind.

August 1931
Helen, Anne, and Polly travel to France and Yugoslavia.

May 1932
The women make a third trip abroad, visiting Scotland and England.

August 26, 1932
John Macy dies in Pennsylvania.

December 1932
Helen is elected to AFB's board of trustees.

June 1933
Helen, Anne, and Polly return to Scotland.

October 20, 1936
Anne Sullivan Macy dies.

November 1936
Helen and Polly travel abroad, visiting England, Scotland, and France.

April 1937
Helen and Polly travel to Japan, Korea, and Manchuria.

Spring 1938
  Helen Keller's Journal, a personal account of Helen's life in 1936 and 1937, is published.

September 1939
  Helen sells her home in Forest Hills, and the household moves to Arcan Ridge in Westport, Connecticut.

January 1943
  Helen begins her visits to the blind, deaf, and disabled soldiers of World War II in military hospitals around the country. She calls this "the crowning experience of my life."

October 1946
  Helen and Polly make their first world tour for the American Foundation for the Overseas Blind (AFOB), AFB's sister organization, visiting London, Paris, Italy, Greece, and Scotland. In the next 11 years, they will visit 35 countries on five continents.

November 1946
  A fire destroys Arcan Ridge, along with almost all of the household's possessions.

September 1947
  The household moves into Arcan Ridge 2, an almost identical replica of the original Arcan Ridge home.

April–August 1948
  Helen and Polly begin a tour of Australia and New Zealand as representatives of the AFOB. When they reach Japan, Polly suffers her first stroke, and the remainder of the tour is canceled.

Chronology

Spring 1950–Spring 1953
Helen and Polly continue to travel all over the world, including Europe, South Africa, the Middle East, and Latin America.

Winter 1953
A documentary film of Helen's life, *The Unconquered* (later renamed *Helen Keller in Her Story*), is released.

February 1955
Helen and Polly embark on a tour of the Far East, including India and Japan.

June 1955
Helen receives an honorary degree from Harvard University, the first woman to be so honored.

December 1955
Teacher, Helen's biography about Anne Sullivan Macy, is published.

Spring 1956
The Unconquered wins an Academy Award for best feature-length documentary of 1955.

November 1956
Helen makes peace with Perkins Institution, attending the dedication of "Keller-Macy Cottage."

Winter 1956–57
William Gibson's play *The Miracle Worker,* based on Helen's early life with Anne, debuts on television and on Broadway.

May 1957
Helen and Polly tour Iceland and Scandinavia.

March 21, 1960
  Polly Thomson dies.

October 1961
  Helen suffers her first stroke and retires from public life.

September 1964
  President Lyndon Johnson confers the Presidential Medal
  of Freedom, the nation's highest civilian honor, upon
  Helen. She is unable to attend the ceremony.

June 1, 1968
  Helen Keller passes away in her sleep. More than 1,200
  mourners attend the funeral at the National Cathedral.
  Helen's ashes are interred there with those of Anne
  and Polly.

This Life

I believe humility is a virtue, but I prefer
not to use it unless it is absolutely necessary.

Brooklyn Eagle, *January 11, 1916*

I wish I might be taken just as a normal person,
and my accomplishments treated
simply as illustrations of how much more
others can do if they only use their five senses
with thought and perseverance.

Letter to Georges L. Raverat, undated

*B*ecause I cannot see or hear, the thoughtless
suppose life must be a blank to me. They do not
understand that things have other precious values
beside color and sound. It never occurs to them
to FEEL a flower, and they do not know what they
miss—the exquisite shape of leaf and stem and bud.
I do not suppose light suggests to them the radiating,
life-giving warmth of the sun. True, I cannot see
the stars scattered like gold-dust in the heavens,
but other stars just as bright shine in my soul.

Letter to Fred Elder, November 21, 1922

*I*f you only knew how exasperated I am by people
who care only about the peculiar sensations
and experiences which they imagine must be mine,
and which must make me different
from themselves. . . . Truly, deafness and blindness
are mere incidents in life—a stage setting
in the great drama of the soul.

Letter to Lord Aberdeen, April 23, 1929

*O*nce I knew the depth where no hope was
and darkness lay on the face of all things.
Then love came and set my soul free.
Once I fretted and beat myself against the wall
that shut me in. My life was without a past or future,
and death a consummation devoutly to be wished.
But a little word from the fingers of another fell
into my hands that clutched at emptiness,
and my heart leaped up with the rapture of living.
I do not know the meaning of the darkness,
but I have learned the overcoming of it.

"Words of Life," Harper, 1966

I may not come and go alone freely, however strong
the lure of the wild or the call of love may be,
yet through imagination a mighty inheritance is mine.
I am heir of all the ages—heir of their wealth of thought
and high endeavor. I am heir of the faith on whose wings
souls mount heavenward and heir of all strength to do
and endure; I am heir of sun and color and harmony.

Letter to Mr. Raymond, undated

I am not a perfect being. . . .
I have more faults than I know what to do with.
I have a naughty temper. I am stubborn, impatient
of hindrances and of stupidity.
I have not in the truest sense a Christian spirit.
I am naturally a fighter. I am lazy.
I put off till tomorrow what I might better do today.
I do not feel that I have been compensated
for the two senses I lack.
I have worked hard for all the senses I have got,
and always I beg for more.

*"A Message from the Hand, or from Darkness to Light
(Another Beginning)," draft of speech, 1928*

I really care for nothing in the world but liberty
in all the departments of life —
liberty to grow mentally and spiritually,
untramelled by tradition and arbitrary standards.

Letter to Dr. Cabot, March 11, 1928

This Life

$\mathcal{Y}$ou see now what I live by—the devotion and
service of others. I was blind, now I see;
I was deaf, now I hear; I was dumb, now I speak,
and it was through the hands of others that
this miracle was wrought in me. It was through
the hands of others that I found myself,
found my mother and father, found the world,
found my soul and love and God. It is through the
hands of others that I, deaf and blind, know the
richness and fulness of life. It is through the strength
of others that I am able to do work that is worth while.

*"A Message from the Hand, or from Darkness to Light
(Another Beginning)," draft of speech, 1928*

$\mathcal{M}$y spirit was indeed in prison before my teacher
came to me. But her love and the power of knowledge
set me free, and I have lived happily in spite
of my deprivations. I am seldom conscious of them,
and I am never really in the dark.

*Letter to Doris and Elsie,
two girls whose mother was deaf-blind, undated*

I dreaded sitting down before a typewriter
and watching the procession of the countless selves
I had been in twenty-five years march from page
to page mocking me. . . . Oh, the mortal hours I sat
while my past selves rose up like spectres and moved
before me, trailing not 'clouds of glory', but thoughts,
feelings and ambitions which looked as forlorn as last
year's bird-nests, and which I scarcely recognized as
things which had once set my heart beating wildly!

Letter to Lord Aberdeen, on writing her autobiography,
April 23, 1929

I am younger today than I was at twenty-five.
Of course the furrows of suffering have been
dug deeper, but so have those of understanding
sympathy and inner happiness. Whatever age may do
to my earthly shell, I shall never grow cynical
or indifferent—and one cannot measure
the reserve power locked up in that assurance.

Letter to Clare Heineman, July 19, 1943

*I*t is perfectly true that my work for the blind is
a trust, and in order to fulfil its duties justly I must
keep it as the centre of my external activities. But it has
never occupied a centre in my personality or inner
relations with mankind. That is because I regard
philanthropy as a tragic apology for wrong conditions
under which human beings live, losing their sight or
hearing or becoming impoverished, and I do not
conceal this awkward position from anybody. . . .
There is an even higher trust—to keep my essential
freedom so that wherever possible I may release
fettered minds and imprisoned lives among the blind,
let alone those who see.

Letter to Nella Braddy, September 18, 1944

*I*hope one day to see enough braille presses,
libraries, schools, and training centers and teachers
to assure all persons the opportunities they would
have had, had they not been blind.
This is my greatest purpose in life.

American Foundation for the Blind greeting card, undated

To Love This Life

*W*hat a strange life I lead—
a kind of Cinderella-life—
half glitter in crystal shoes, half mice and cinders!
But it is a wonderful life all the same.

Letter to Mrs. Felix [Carrie] Fuld, ca. 1933

———•———

*S*ometimes a sense of isolation enfolds me
like a mist. But I no longer feel I stand alone. . . .
So much has been given me I have no time
to ponder over that which has been denied.

"Helen Keller at 80," interview by Ann Carnahan,
This Week Magazine, *June 19, 1960*

The Senses

*U*se your eyes as if tomorrow you would be
stricken blind. . . . Hear the music of voices,
the song of the bird, the mighty strains of an orchestra,
as if you would be stricken deaf tomorrow.
Touch each object as if tomorrow your tactile sense
would fail. Smell the perfume of the flowers,
taste with relish each morsel,
as if tomorrow you could
never smell and taste again.
Make the most of every sense;
glory in all the facets of pleasure and beauty
which the world reveals to you.

"Three Days to See," Atlantic Monthly, *January 1933*

*P*eople wonder that I know joy and contentment
when the wide realm of sunlight, color, song
and laughter is barred against me.
Well, I have always observed that those
who express surprise at my enjoyment of life
are those who use their senses imperfectly.

*"A Message from the Hand, or from Darkness to Light
(Another Beginning)," draft of speech, 1928*

*L*ight is like thought—a bright, amazing thing
perceived by the eyes of the mind.
I am conscious of an infinite variety of images,
relations and degrees of brightness and darkness,
void and fulness, space, height, depth
and conceptual harmonies which I transmute
into sound and color.

Letter to Elmer Ambrose Sperry, February 27, 1930

The Senses

I can tell music from other vibrations by its rhythm
and—I have no touch-word for its velvety singing
through me. I detect loud and soft tones,
swelling chords and dance measures.
Each musical instrument has its own quality
of vibration. A violin sings or sobs into my hand
like the human voice. The music of the organ rolls,
thunders, sinks as if into the sea, mounts upward
and sweeps out into space carrying my soul
on its majestic wings. The wild call of the bugle
is unlike the insistent beat of the drum
or the sweetness of the harp.

Letter to Mr. Sagendorph, April 26, 1935

I think people do not usually realize what
an extensive apparatus the sense of touch is. . . .
Every particle of the skin is a feeler which touches
and is touched and gives contact,
which enables the mind to draw conclusions.

"I Am Blind, I Am Deaf—Yet I See—Yet I Hear,"
The American Magazine, *June 1929*

I have experienced marvelously the qualities
of the spirit in the hand during my dark, silent life.
For it is my hand that binds me to humanity.

"Magic In Your Fingers!"
The Home Magazine, *May 1932*

***

*S*mell is a precious contact with the outside world.
It tells me of a multitude of objects
beyond the reach of my finger-tips.
Everything has its own odor, which is its soul—
tree, flower, soil, rain, burning wood.

"A Neglected Treasure," The Home Magazine, *June 1934*

***

W. H. Hudson says, 'What we see, we feel.'
With me, it is the other way around;
what I feel, I see.

"I Am Blind, I Am Deaf—Yet I See—Yet I Hear,"
The American Magazine, *June 1929*

*I*f I, deaf, blind, find life rich and interesting,
how much more can you gain by the use
of your five senses!

*"A Message from the Hand, or from Darkness to Light
(Another Beginning)," draft of speech, 1928*

~·~

*D*o you wonder that I love the hand?
I have felt its glorious power to love, to redeem,
to do the work of the world.
All that is noble and generous and creative
in the human race has come to me
through the hand.

"Helen Keller's Address to the Blind of New York City,"
Outlook for the Blind, *Winter 1913*

~·~

*T*he most beautiful world is always entered
through imagination.

The World I Live In, *1908*

*W*hen I consider all the delights the sense of smell
brings me, I am amazed that this most intimate sense
should be so generally neglected. . . .
The nose is as complex as the eye or the ear,
and as well equipped for the acquisition of knowledge,
but to speak of educating the nose
provokes only a smile.

"A *Neglected Treasure*," The Home Magazine, *June 1934*

~•~

*I*n all I do and think, I am conscious of a hand.
People dependent upon their eyes and ears seldom
understand the wealth of life that is tangible.

"*The World Through Three Senses*,"
Ladies Home Journal, *March 1951*

The Senses

*W*e differ, blind and seeing,
not in the nature of our handicap,
but in the understanding and idealism
we put into the art of living.
It is only when we put imagination and feeling
behind the senses
that they attain their full value.

Speech for the Twentieth Century Club, 1922

Faith is the strength by which a shattered world shall emerge into the light

Helen Keller

Faith

*M*y own mind rebels against skepticism and denial,
and responds with joy and eagerness
only to indomitable faith and hope.

Letter to Fred Elder, November 21, 1922

*W*hen we complain of having to do the same thing
over and over, let us remember that God does not send
new trees, strange flowers and different grasses
every year. When the spring winds blow, they blow
in the same way. In the same places the same dear
blossoms lift up the same sweet faces, yet they never
weary us. When it rains, it rains as it always has.
Even so would the same tasks which fill our daily lives
put on new meanings if we wrought them in the spirit
of renewal from within—a spirit of growth and beauty.

An Easter Message to the Boston Community Church, 1932

*T*here is, I am convinced, a correspondence
between the powers of the body
and those of the spirit;
the senses serve as entrances to an inner world.

"The World Through Three Senses,"
Ladies Home Journal, *March 1951*

❧

*F*aith is a mockery if it does not teach us
that we can build a more complete
and beautiful world.

"My New Speech," undated

❧

*W*hen I hear people talking about faith,
I am not content, I want them to go and do
what they believe at all times, in the market
just as heartily as in the parlor.

*"A Message from the Hand, or from Darkness to Light
(Another Beginning)," draft of speech, 1928*

Faith

It was a terrible blow to my faith when I learned
that millions of my fellow-creatures must labor all
their days for food and shelter, bear the most crushing
burdens and die without having known the joy
of living. My security vanished forever, and I have
never regained the radiant belief of my young years
that earth is a happy home and hearth
for the majority of mankind. But faith is
a state of mind. The believer is not soon disheartened.
If he is turned out of his shelter, he builds up a house
that the winds of the earth cannot destroy.

"The Light of a Brighter Day," broadcast on
This I Believe, *radio show of Edward R. Murrow, ca. 1951*

Character is like the fire within the flint—latent
until it is struck out of the stone. Observing the flint
stone, who would think it contained the possibility
of light? And so it is with the dark experiences of life.
When they are met with courage,
they give out sparks of spiritual light.

"We Who Sit Apart," Outlook for the Blind, *March 1924*

*T*rue faith is not a fruit of security,
it is the ability to blend mortal fragility
with the inner strength of the Spirit.
It does not shift with the changing shades
of one's thought.

"The Light of a Brighter Day," broadcast on
This I Believe, *radio show of Edward R. Murrow, ca. 1951*

*L*ife without faith is uneasy, timorous,
and wholly spent in running away
from misfortunes which are
in the nature of things inescapable.

We Bereaved, *1929*

Happiness

When one door of happiness closes, another opens;
but often we look so long at the closed door
that we do not see the one
which has been opened for us.

We Bereaved, *1929*

Happiness is a state of mind,
and depends very little
on outward circumstances.

Speech to fellow passengers
on the S.S. President Roosevelt, October 1, 1930

*N*othing of value can be done without joy.
Cultivate happiness in yourself and in others,
and you will wonder at the beauty, the richness,
the power that come to you
through your bright spirit.

"My New Speech," undated

—❖—

*I*t is said that success is happiness. I think good-will
and service to all men are the true kind of happiness.
They are things that endure. They bring riches
that never pass away,
and happiness that never fails.

*Speech to fellow passengers
on the S.S. President Roosevelt, October 1, 1930*

—❖—

*W*e are never really happy until we try
to brighten the lives of others.

"My New Speech," undated

I take happiness very seriously. It is a creed, a
philosophy and an objective.

"Happiness," School Bank News
*[published by the East New York Savings Bank,
Brooklyn, NY], May 1935*

---

*U*sefulness, I believe,
is the highest joy of man's life.

*Letter to Colonel Edwin A. Baker,
Director of the National Institute for the Blind,
Toronto, Canada, undated*

---

*R*eality even when it is sad
is better than illusions. Illusions are at the mercy
of any winds that blow. Real happiness must come
from within, from a fixed purpose
and faith in one's fellow men.

Interview by Barbara Bentley,
New York Tribune, *January 16, 1916*

To Love This Life

*S*ome people are foolish enough to imagine
that wealth and power and fame satisfy our hearts:
but they never do, unless they are used
to create and distribute happiness in the world.

*Thank-you letter to Daniel, son of a donor,
who also contributed part of his allowance,
February 17, 1926*

◆

I believe God gave us life for happiness
not misery. And I believe that happiness,
attained, should be shared.

"Helen Keller at 80," interview by Ann Carnahan,
This Week Magazine, *June 19, 1960*

◆

*I*f we do not like our work, and do not try
to get happiness out of it, we are a menace
to our profession as well as to ourselves.

"Know Thyself,"
The Home Magazine, *September 1930*

Friendship and Love

*C*ultivate love for love is the light that gives the eye
to see great and noble things.

"Helen Keller at 80," interview by Ann Carnahan,
This Week Magazine, *June 19, 1960*

*T*he best and most beautiful thing in life
is friendship that springs out of the heart,
as fragrances out of the flower. It is all the color
and music of my world of dark silence.

Letter to Mrs. Joy Bourne, October 28, 1930

*T*he heart of a friend gives out sufficient light
for us in the dark to rise by.

Inscription in a copy of Midstream
presented to Craig B. Hazelwood, November 1930

~•~

*M*y life is 'a chronicle of friendship.'
My friends—all those about me—
create my world anew each day.
Without their loving care,
all the courage I could summon would not suffice
to keep my heart strong for life.

Midstream, *1930*

~•~

I am not conscious of my friends'—or of other
people's physical deficiencies.
My mind instinctively dwells upon
their beautiful capabilities of mind and heart.

Letter to Fred Elder, November 21, 1922

Friendship and Love

*W*hen I recollect the treasure of friendship
that has been bestowed upon me I withdraw
all charges against life. If much has been denied me,
much, very much has been given.
So long as the memory of certain beloved friends
lives in my heart I shall say that life is good.

Midstream, *1930*

❧

*A*nalysis is as destructive of emotion
as of the flower which the botanist pulls to pieces.

Midstream, *1930*

❧

*T*he best and most beautiful things in the world
cannot be seen nor even touched,
but just felt in the heart.

Letter to Reverend Phillips Brooks,
South Boston, June 8, 1891

Life and Living

*T*here is just one way to make sure of immortality,
and that is to love this life and live it
as richly and helpfully as we can.

"Deeds of Immortality,"
The Home Magazine, *June 1935*

*L*ife is either a daring adventure or nothing.
To keep our faces toward change and behave
like free spirits in the presence of fate
is strength undefeatable.

Let Us Have Faith, *1941*

*L*ife is made up of joy and sorrow,
and in the long run we all get our share of each.

"O! Brave New World That Has Such People In't,"
Red Cross Magazine, *September 1919*

---

*L*ife is an exciting business
and most exciting when it is lived for others.

Quoted in Contemporary Quotations,
*compiled by James B. Simpson, Thomas Y. Crowell,
1964, p. 312, from news report of June 26, 1955*

---

*U*nless we can help the world where we are,
we could not help it if we were somewhere else.
The most important thing is not the kind
of environment we have, but the kind of thoughts
we think every day, the kind of ideals we are following.

*Speech delivered at the Kent Street Reformed Church,
Brooklyn, NY, 1927*

*I*f we don't make the most of ourselves,
how can we expect to be made much of by others?

Address to blinded WWI soldiers,
delivered at Evergreen Hospital, Baltimore, MD,
February 25, 1919.
Published in Evergreen Review, *April 1920*

❧

*I*t is not required of every man and woman
to do or be something great.
Most of us have to be content to take small parts
in the drama of life.

An Easter Message to the Boston Community Church, 1932

❧

*W*hat really counts in life is the quiet meeting
of every difficulty with the determination
to get out of it all the good there is.

"Know Thyself," The Home Magazine, *September 1930*

*G*od has given each one of us a task,
which we can perform better
than anyone else. We must find out
what that task is,
and how to do it in the best way possible.

Letter to Friends, March 30, 1921

---

*W*hen people are old enough to write their memoirs,
it is time for them to die, it seems to me.
It would save themselves and others
a great deal of trouble if they did.

Midstream, 1929

---

*E*ach new experience in life is an encounter.
There is a struggle—a cloud of dust,
and we come out of it wiser,
and perhaps a little bit crestfallen.

Letter to Andrew and Louise Carnegie, April 21, 1913

Life and Living

*L*ife is more cruel than death
for life divides and estranges.

"Helen Keller at 80," interview by Ann Carnahan,
This Week Magazine, *June 19, 1960*

—•—

*I*t seemed more strange than ever that death
should cause fear when one is endowed with the power
mentally to survey such a supremely magnificent
universe evolving out of chaos! Since each galaxy
discovered is another proof of change,
why cannot death be life in another form?

Letter to Robert and Mathilde Pfeiffer, undated

—•—

*T*omorrow! What possibilities there are in that word.
No matter how discouraging today, how gloomy
with dark clouds, with terrors and illness and death,
there's always Tomorrow, with its promise
of better things. Let us think then of Death
as but one more tomorrow,
filled with infinite promise and fulfillment.

We Bereaved, *1929*

Education

The highest result of education is tolerance.
Long ago men fought and died for their faith;
but it took ages to teach them the other kind
of courage—the courage to recognize the faiths
of their brethren and their rights of conscience.
Tolerance is the first principle of community;
it is the spirit that conserves the best
that all men think. No loss by flood and lightning,
no destruction of cities and temples by the hostile force
of nature, has deprived man of so many noble lives
as those which his intolerance has destroyed.

My Key of Life, 1926

*T*rue education combines intellect, beauty,
goodness, and the greatest of these is goodness.

Out of the Dark, *1907*

—•—

*E*ducation should train the child to use his brains,
to make for himself a place in the world
and maintain his rights even when it seems
that society would shove him into the scrap-heap.

"*Going Back to School,*"
The Home Magazine, *September 1934*

—•—

I cannot but say a word and look my disapproval
when I hear that my country is spending millions
for war and war engines—more, I have heard,
than twice as much as the entire public school system
costs the nation.

"*My Future as I See It,*"
Metropolitan Magazine, *1904*

*E*ducation is not simply teaching people
things they do not know, but rather teaching them
to behave as they do not behave.
By that I mean teaching them to unfold
the natural sympathies of the heart,
which we seldom permit to
manifest themselves in acts.

Speech, Philadelphia, April 20, 1931

*T*he education of today tends
to make us chauvinistic.
It emphasizes class and nation and individualism.
We are taught that competition is essential
to the health and progress of the race. . . .
I maintain that cooperation is good,
and competition is bad, that society does not flourish
by the antagonism of its atoms,
but by the mutual helpfulness of human beings.

Speech, Philadelphia, April 20, 1931

*W*hat do I consider a teacher should be?
One who breathes life into knowledge
so that it takes new form
in progress and civilization.

Speech to the National Education Association, 1938

*T*rue teaching cannot be learned
from text-books any more than a surgeon
can acquire his skill by reading about surgery.

Letter to Kathern Gruber, November 1, 1955

*W*hat induces a child to learn
but his delight in knowing?

My Religion, *1927*

Education

*I*f the most wonderful of all God's Works
is the human individual,
surely the richness with which
He endows the teacher must be
the supreme miracle of creative ingenuity.

Telegram to Professor John Dewey on his 70th birthday, 1929

Books and Literature

*M*ore than at any other time,
when I hold a beloved book in my hand
my limitations fall from me, my spirit is free.

Midstream, *1930*

A special affection binds me to Poets
because the magic of their words snatches away
my dark silence as a veil, and I find myself
flooded with light and harmony. All creation
escorts me on my way as I walk with the Poets.

Letter to Mr. Hillyer, undated

*L*iterature is my Utopia.
Here I am not disenfranchised.
No barrier of the senses shuts me out from the sweet,
gracious discourse of my book-friends.
They talk to me without embarrassment
or awkwardness.

The Story of My Life, *1902*

❧

*E*very book put into the hands of the sightless
is as a rainbow crystal that reveals
the wonders of earth and the spiritual resources
within our reach.

Letter to Louise Carnegie [wife of Andrew Carnegie],
January 11, 1930

❧

*W*hen a poet speaks he covers the bare facts
of life with a shimmering cloth of gold.
He spiritualizes all that men see, feel, think, suffer,
learn of life's heights and depths.

Introduction to Arrows in the Gale, *by Arturo Giovannitti,*
Hillacre Bookhouse, Riverside, CT, 1914

Books and Literature

A book that fills the mind with beauty
and opens the heart
to what is lovely and lovable in an alien civilization
is a treasure forever.

Letter to Miss Lord, Autumn 1933

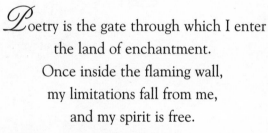

*P*oetry is the gate through which I enter
the land of enchantment.
Once inside the flaming wall,
my limitations fall from me,
and my spirit is free.

Letter to Edward Morgan, February 13, 1921

Nature

*W*hat life can be more satisfying than to think
high thoughts undisturbed and steep one's spirit
in the strong, simple wisdom of nature's ways?

Letter to Mrs. Barclay, April 9, 1931

*P*eople often express surprise that
I can enjoy nature when I cannot see its beauties
or hear its harmonies. But really it is they
who are blind. For they have no idea how fair
the flower is to the touch, nor do they appreciate
its fragrance, which is the soul of the flower.

Letter to Miss Bose in India, December 10, 1923

I have great joy in the tulips and lilacs
which make my garden 'look like the waking
of Creation.' O the potent wichery of smell!
Leaves opening delicately on tree and rambler
and rose-bush tell me God has passed this way,
and I forget the disturbing nearness of the city
in the eternal miracle of a tiny garden
great with wonders.

Letter to Waldo Mac Eagar of the
British Empire Society for the Blind, May 13, 1933

I am thankful that in a troubled world
no calamity can prevent the return of spring.

Letter to Mrs. Felix [Carrie] Fuld, May 10, 1933

*A*ll my life flowers have spoken to me
with a language delicate
beyond human utterance.

Letter to Mrs. E. Kearne, April 7, 1948

Nature

I cannot hear the orchestra of bird voices
in my garden, but the trees and flowers
amaze me with their endless changes.
The pines drop pitch upon my hand,
and I know that summer is near.

"The World Through Three Senses,"
Ladies Home Journal, *March 1951*

Women in Society

*W*e have prayed, we have coaxed,
we have begged, for the vote,
with the hope that men, out of chivalry,
would bestow equal rights upon women
and take them into partnership in the affairs
of the state. We hoped that their common sense
would triumph over prejudices and stupidity.
We thought their boasted sense of justice
would overcome the errors that so often
fetter the human spirit; but we have always
gone away empty handed.
We shall beg no more.

Speech to the delegates of the New Woman's Party,
June 11, 1916, Chicago

I am deaf; but I hear the glad tidings
of woman's liberation which shall soon be flung abroad
through the land. I am blind; but I see
the dawning light of a new day when there shall be
no woman enslaved, no child robbed of the sweet joy
of childhood in the war of daily bread.

Undelivered speech for suffrage,
prepared for Washington, DC, March 3, 1913

━•━

*E*very child has a right to be well-born,
well-nurtured and well-taught,
and only the freedom of woman
can guarantee him this right.

Undelivered speech for suffrage,
prepared for Washington, DC, March 3, 1913

━•━

*T*he woman who works for a dollar a day
has as much right as any other human being
to say what the conditions of her work should be.

"The Modern Woman. 1. The Educated Woman,"
Metropolitan Magazine, *October 1912*

Women in Society

$\mathcal{T}$here are no such things as divine, immutable
or inalienable rights. Rights are things
we get when we are strong enough
to make good our claim to them.

"Why Men Need Women Suffrage,"
New York Call, *October 17, 1915*

—•—

$\mathcal{W}$e women have the privilege of going hungry
while our men are in battle, and it is our right
to be widowed and orphaned by political stupidity
and economic chaos.

"The Modern Woman. 1. The Educated Woman,"
Metropolitan Magazine, *October 1912*

—•—

$\mathcal{I}$ have no patience with women who say,
'Oh, I can't do anything about solving this problem.
Time adjusts all things.' That is not true.
Wrong things cannot work themselves right. We,
ourselves, must always work them right.

"Crushing Out Our Children's Lives,"
The Home Magazine, *August 1931*

*N*ever in the history of the world has woman
held a position of such dignity, honour,
and usefulness as now. . . . I think the degree
of a nation's civilisation may be measured
by the degree of enlightenment of its women.

"*My Future as I See It*," Metropolitan Magazine, 1904

❧

*L*et women once join together in demanding
and building up for world unity and peace
as a condition of their own well-being and the safety
of their children's children, and their mission will
indeed be fulfilled as creators and preservers
of the human race.

Letter to Elisabeth Trippmacher, 1947

❧

I believe that world peace is the mission
of woman—the wheel she must lay
on the anvil and shape to her desire.

Speech honoring Jane Addams, New York, December 6, 1929

*W*e women have to face questions that men alone
have evidently not been quite able to solve.
We must know why a woman who owns property
has no voice in selecting the men who make laws
that affect her property. We must know
why a woman who earns wages has nothing to say
about the choice of the men who make laws
that govern her wages. We must know
why a hundred and fifty of our sisters were killed
in New York in a shirt-waist factory fire the other day,
and nobody to blame. We must know why
our fathers, brothers and husbands are killed
in mines and on railroads. We women,
who are natural conservationists,
must find out why the sons we bring forth
are drawn up in line and shot.

"The Modern Woman. 1. The Educated Woman,"
Metropolitan Magazine, *October 1912*

Human Nature

*I*nsensibility is the only hopeless darkness.

Letter to Ginn O'Hara, July 24, 1956

❧

*I*t is easier to teach [the blind] to see
the beauty of the universe than to teach ignorance
to think and insensibility to feel.
Many people with perfect ears are emotionally deaf,
many with splendid eyes are blind in their perceptions.

Speech for the Twentieth Century Club, 1922

*B*lind and deaf as I am, I get more fun
out of life than a lot of people I know
who think they see, but they are as blind as bats
when it comes to understanding.

Address to blinded WWI soldiers,
delivered at Evergreen Hospital, Baltimore, MD,
February 25, 1919.
Published in Evergreen Review, *April 1920*

‑•‑

*O*nly in quietness do we possess our own minds
and discover the resources of the Inner Life.

"The Beauty of Silence," The Home Magazine, *May 1935*

‑•‑

*T*he world needs more of this dauntless
spirit of laughter. Laughter is more disconcerting
than a whole dictionary of abuse.

Impromptu remarks at the "Good-Morning" dinner,
November 6, 1920

*M*any people never stop to think what life means.
They hurry and scurry, they run to and fro
upon the earth, exploring the paths
that lead nowhere. They waste their energies
in futile attempts that gain nothing.
It is as if they tried to lift themselves up
by their waistbands or to walk on their heads.
Not until Fate, or Destiny, or some other fellow
knocks them out, do they learn to look
within themselves for happiness.

Address to blinded WWI soldiers,
delivered at Evergreen Hospital, Baltimore, MD,
February 25, 1919.
Published in Evergreen Review, *April 1920*

⚊•⚊

*E*verybody talks, nobody listens. . . .
Good listeners are as rare as white crows.

"The Beauty of Silence," The Home Magazine, *May 1935*

*C*haracter cannot be developed in ease and quiet.
Helen Keller's Journal, *1938*

—•—

*E*very decisive act, I believe,
must be clearly thought out
as well as good-intentioned. Want of intelligent
thinking is as harmful as lack of heart.
Letter to Jo Davidson, 1948

—•—

*I*t is wonderful how much time good people spend
fighting the devil. If they would only spend
the same amount of energy loving their fellow men,
the devil would die in his own tracks of ennui.
Quoted in A. L. Alexander's
Treasurehouse of Inspirational Poetry and Prose,
Doubleday & Co., Garden City, New York, 1966.

*H*umility and resignation
are virtues I don't particularly admire.

*Address delivered during July/August 1916
on the Midland Chautauqua Circuit*

I have always felt great repugnance
for the publicity that dogs the acts
of one who happens to be different
from the crowd.

Letter to Lady Nancy Astor, June 12, 1933

---

*B*lind people are just like seeing people
in the dark. The loss of sight does not impair
the qualities of mind and heart.

Speech at a church, 1951

War and Peace

*W*ar is a beast that devours civilization
and turns all good works to contempt.
Kings and governments make war.
The people pay the cost.

*Address for the British, French, Belgian Permanent Blind
Relief Fund, New York City, June 21, 1916*

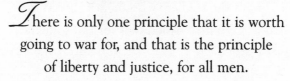

*T*here is only one principle that it is worth
going to war for, and that is the principle
of liberty and justice, for all men.

Address to Soldiers, Camp Vail, Little Silver Spring, 1918

I think the truly brave and strong desire peace,
and feel that peace has victories more glorious
than any that the sword has won.

Letter to Adolfos Mehlisch, October 27, 1905

I grow more and more suspicious
of the political powers that take men away
from their work and set them shooting one another.

The Modern Woman. 1. The Educated Woman,
Metropolitan Magazine, October 1912

---

*S*urely, the appalling waste of modern war
and the scanty returns it makes in comparison
to those who wage it must become
more and more apparent. Indeed, now it is not
so much the soldiers who die for the country
as the country which dies for the soldiers.

Letter to Henry Ford, November 30, 1915

War and Peace

*W*e cannot lead the nations in the way
they should go while we tolerate
the crime of lynching,
the crime of child-labor,
the crime of poverty.
We cannot guide the world toward peace
if we arm ourselves
and play the bully over our weaker neighbors.

*"America Against War," speech delivered
during July/August 1916
on the Midland Chautauqua Circuit*

*W*hat can rulers, nobility and all the lords
of the earth say to justify the horrible killing
and maiming of twenty or thirty million
valuable men who a short while ago ploughed,
dug, wove, built, guided the traffic of the world,
took their pleasure, loved their fellows,
cherished their families,
and feared naught?

Letter to Henry Ford, November 30, 1915

*W*ar is negation of life, blasphemy.
So long as men are murdered, and go forth to murder,
and employ their peaceful years in preparing
tools of murder, the Gospels and the Prophets
and the Law are an insult and a mockery.

A Christmas Appeal, 1917

~•~

*P*eace and prosperity will come
when we realize, and incorporate into our lives
the truth that we live by each other
and for each other
and not unto ourselves.

*Speech delivered Armistice Day, November 11, 1931,
Pearl River High School, under the auspices
of the Rockland County Peace Association*

Changing the World

I do not like the world as it is; so I am trying to make it a little more as I want it.

"A Message from the Hand, or from Darkness to Light (Another Beginning)," draft of speech, 1928

I, for one, love strength, daring, fortitude. I do not want people to kill the fight in them; I want them to fight for right things.

Address delivered during July/August 1916 on the Midland Chautauqua Circuit

*I*nstead of being satisfied to alleviate suffering,
we shall labor hard and continually to prevent it.

"Facing the Future," speech, 1916

❧

*H*istory is a record of the incessant struggle
of humanity against ignorance and oppression.

"The Age of Labor," draft of speech, January 12, 1918

❧

*S*ometimes people say that I must be happy
because I live in a beautiful dream,
away from the discord and sorrow of the world.
I did once; but now the dream is gone forever.
With eyes wide open I see how bare and harsh
life is for the greater part of my fellowmen,
and I suffer with them.

"My New Speech," undated

*N*o one has ever given me a good reason
why we should obey unjust laws. But the reason
why we should resist them is obvious. . . .
The dignity of human nature compels us
to resist what we believe to be wrong
and a stumbling block to our fellowmen.
When a government puts forth its strength
on the side of injustice it is foredoomed to fail.

Introduction to Arrows in the Gale, *by Arturo Giovannitti,*
1914, Hillacre Bookhouse, Riverside, CT

———— ·—

*O*nly people count. Only people who think
and feel and work together make civilization.
Only governments that keep every door of opportunity
wide open are civilized governments. . . .
Civilization means a fair chance to live.
It means an equitable share of the resources
of the earth for every one. It means health
and freedom and education for all men.

"The Russian Revolution," draft of speech, June 1918

*E*very one of us is blind and deaf until our eyes
are opened to our fellowmen,
until our ears hear the voice of humanity.

*"A Message from the Hand, or from Darkness to Light
(Another Beginning)," draft of speech, 1928*

*T*here are plenty of senses and plenty of brains
in the world if we put them together
and work together. We can, we shall,
we must repair each other's misfortunes
and the gross, unnecessary misfortunes of mankind.

*"A Message from the Hand, or from Darkness to Light
(Another Beginning)," draft of speech, 1928*

*A*gain and again down through the ages
humanity has shown itself equal
to its dream of justice.

"The Russian Revolution," draft of speech, June 1918

*H*e who is content with what has been done
is an obstacle in the path of progress.

Speech to the Massachusetts Association
for the Promotion of the Interests of the Blind, June 1927

❧

*T*he heart of the world is wrung
when a great ship like the Titanic
goes to the bottom freighted with human lives.
But we scarcely notice the far greater wreck
of human lives in the daily war for bread.

"A Message from the Hand, or from Darkness to Light
(Another Beginning)," draft of speech, 1928

❧

*P*overty is the fundamental cause
of most of the physical, moral
and economic ills of humanity.

"A Letter to You from Helen Keller,"
letter for the American Association
for the Conservation of Vision,
October 30, 1911

*I*t is no true optimism to declare
that the world is a good world when it is not.
It is for us rather to insist that it shall be made good,
and exert ourselves to bring it about.

"*My New Speech,*" *undated*

———•———

*R*evolution means transformation,
and is accomplished when an entirely new principle
is put in the place of existing things. . . .
Reform aims only at improvement, or more logical
or just consequences. Reform may be effected
with bloodshed. Revolution may take place
in the most profound tranquility.

"*The Age of Labor,*" *draft of speech, January 12, 1918*

———•———

*T*here is no blindness more insidious,
more fatal than this race for profit, or competition.

"*A Message from the Hand, or from Darkness to Light
(Another Beginning),*" *draft of speech, 1928*

$\mathcal{T}$he test of a democracy is not the magnificence
of buildings or the speed of automobiles
or the efficiency of air transportation, but rather
the care given to the welfare of all the people.

"*Try Democracy,*" The Home Magazine, *April 1935*

———•———

$\mathcal{O}$ur democracy is but a name. We vote? What does
that mean? It means that we choose between
two bodies of real, though not avowed autocrats.
We choose between Tweedledum and Tweedledee.

*Letter to Mrs. Grindon, January 12, 1911, published
in the Manchester [England] Advertiser, March 3, 1911*

———•———

$\mathcal{N}$o nation is wise enough to rule another.
That is why empires have fallen
and are still falling.

Let Us Have Faith, *1941*

*W*e are already on the road to success . . .
when we see that because we have always
done something, and because everybody does it,
and because our grandfathers did it,
are not good reasons why we should do it.

Introduction to My Religion

❖

*A*nyone who will take a peep
into life's backyard will see a huge junk heap
that will set him thinking.

Birth Control, New York Call, November 26, 1915

❖

*T*he civilization of a state should be measured
by the amount of suffering it prevents
and the degree of happiness it makes possible
for its citizens.

*Speech to the legislature of Iowa on a bill
to create a commission for the blind,
Des Moines, 1927*

*S*ociety declared that no man should be enslaved,
and the feudal system fell. Society declared
that no man should be ignorant, and the power
of ecclesiastical despotism was broken. Now society
is about to declare that no man shall be exploited
for the benefit of another man; for then
he cannot be truly free.

"The Age of Labor," draft of speech, January 12, 1918

*T*he attempt to suppress an idea
has always and everywhere
proved a failure.

*"Dr. Haiselden's Service to Society
in Allowing the Bollenger Baby to Die,"
written for International News Service, undated*

*T*he power of effecting changes for the better
is within ourselves, not in the favorableness
of circumstances.

"Rehabilitation," October 31, 1923

People and Events

On Anne Sullivan Macy

*E*ver since she took my hand
on the door-step of my home,
she has been not only my eyes and ears,
but also a light in all dark places,
a bond between me
and the life of the world.

Letter to Henry Ford, September 9, 1922

On Alexander Graham Bell
---

*H*e explained to me how the telephone worked.
One evening while we were waiting for a streetcar,
beside a telephone pole, he placed my hand on the
weather-smoothed wood and said,
'Feel. What do the vibrations mean to you? Anything?'
I had never put my hand on a pole before.
He said that the humming which I felt in my fingers
never stopped, that the copper wires above us
were carrying the messages of birth and death,
war and finance, failure and success from station
to station round the world. . . . The telephone is one
of the most far-reaching achievements of our time.
But it is not the fact that Dr. Bell invented it which
gives him a living hold on my heart today. It is the fact
that all his life he loved the deaf, and tried in every way
to break down their prison-walls and place them
in touch with the pleasant social ways of mankind.
No matter what else occupied his thoughts,
he never forgot that the chief end and aim of his life
was to teach the deaf to speak.

Speech to the Telephone Pioneers of America,
Boston, MA, November 3, 1928

On Enrico Caruso

*O*ne of my very precious memories is that
of the spring day in Atlanta when you sang for me.
God loved me on that day, Signor Caruso.
Do you recall the day—the soft air,
the smell of wild azaleas, the dogwood trees
along the city streets, like a procession of brides
with white veils? You were as genial and kindly
as the southern sunshine. I still thrill at the recollection
of the Samson Aria. As I pressed my fingers
to your lips, I felt the voice behind them quicken
and throb, as if eager to burst into song.

Letter to Enrico Caruso, July 2, 1918

On Mark Twain

*H*ow I loved Mark Twain when I,
a girl of fourteen, met him in New York!
It was a joy to me simply to be in the same room
with him, he was so beautiful!
His presence shone with the light of his spirit,
and he had the unconscious grace and majesty
of a Greek god. As I grew older, I realized
more and more that he was a great American,
a Great human being. I marvelled when he talked,
and I felt the power of his mind—broad, splendid,
exuberant as the Mississippi he loved.

Letter to E. D. Fulton, August 3, 1920

—◆—

*M*ark Twain was the embodiment
of a burning soul. His every gesture and word
had sparkle, grace and distinction.
He gave me a thrill—and a thrill
is the most exquisite thing one can give another.
I still feel the spell of his exciting personality

after thirty years. When his name appears
on a page under my hand, a quiver
of expectancy runs through me.
My fingers dash over the lines eager to read
whatever there is about him. . . .

The simplest fact,
when his imagination touched it,
glowed as full of meaning as a star is freighted
with light. Life and living interested him tremendously.
He entered into my limited world
with enthusiasm just as he might have
explored Mars. Blindness was an adventure that
kindled his curiosity. He treated me
not as a freak but as a handicapped woman
seeking a way to circumvent
extraordinary difficulties.
There was something of divine apprehension
in this so rare naturalness towards those
who differ from others in external circumstances.

"The Hundredth Anniversary
of Mark Twain's Birth: A Tribute," November 13, 1935

On the Zeppelin

$\mathcal{T}$he people in the street began shouting:—
'There it is! There it is! Look!
Up there! The Zeppelin!'
We hurried out into the garden,
and there it was—my friend could see it distinctly,
sautering [sic] gracefully in the morning sky. . . .
I could not see it with my physical eyes;
but my spirit sensed its deeper significance;
the Kingdom of God on earth is not a dream;
it is the thing before us, the inevitable destiny
of mankind. We have been led
through the dark jungle of war to the conquest
of a new and nobler civilization.
This shining ship of the air is a pledge
of peace against the confusion
and evil of the world.

Letter to Otto Kahn, October 15, 1924

On listening to the radio

*E*ven I derive great pleasure from touching one
and feeling rhythmic vibrations. . . . I think of the radio
as a wonderful voice from the outside world
which binds closer together those who see
and those who cannot see—as a messenger of sympathy
and aid, a consoler of the lonely, an enlarger
of the common life, a carrier of news
and knowledge, a scatterer of sunshine.

*Letter to Atwater Kent, March 1929, asking for a donation
of radios for the American Foundation for the Blind
to send to blind people*

*I*t is a perpetual wonder to me how the voices
that slumber in musical instruments wake and come
to my fingers through that master instrument
of yours. . . . By merely turning a little disc, winter
is transformed into a midsummer night's dream! . . .
O how I love my radio! My joy is multiplied tenfold
by the pleasure of those who 'listen in' with me.

Letter to Atwater Kent, February 26, 1931

On climbing the Acropolis

$\mathcal{T}$he hotel in Athens where we stayed was only
a short distance from the Acropolis, which we saw
at dawn and at sunset. Before my ascent I found
a fallen pillar of Zeus and carefully followed its length
to the top, so that when I touched the columns
of the Parthenon, I could imagine its loveliness
as a whole. While I stood beside the Parthenon,
I wondered at the engineering of the Greeks
and the combination of grace with sheer skill.
It seemed for a moment that the ancient world
had then attained beauty, unity and equilibrium.
I remembered the Pyramids whose stones were full
of slave-labor, whip-pain, blood and tears, and I
shuddered. But the Parthenon poured its healing upon
me, and as we looked down from the summit upon the
Agora where Pericles had counselled the people, I knew
that democracy had begun its struggle there. No, we
have never been left without lights to guide our efforts.
. . . I know the Acropolis as a great symbol
of what obstacles the handicapped may conquer.

Letter to Selma Ettlinger, undated

On the aftermath of World War I

*W*e entered the World War in 1917,
blindly following those who told us that it was a war
to end war, that it would make the world safe
for democracy, that it would secure little nations
against the aggression of great ones. We see now that
those who fought for these principles gave their lives
in vain. There is less democracy in the world
than ever. The little nations are still at the mercy
of their powerful neighbors.

"Memorial Day Thoughts,"
marked "original mailed New York, January 11, 1934"

On the persecution of the Jews in Germany

*M*y heart is full of indignant sorrow as I read
of the barbarities to the Jews being perpetrated
in Germany. It seems unbelievable that a race which
has produced Spinosa, Einstein and Karl Marx should
be persecuted as they were in the Dark Ages!

Letter to Mrs. Felix [Carrie] Fuld, May 10, 1933

On the Warsaw Ghetto Memorial

*I*t was spiritually a day of tempest
and heart-searchings for me when I entered
your studio on the 23rd of October, and with a creator's
authority you placed my hand on a sculpture that
lovers of mankind will sanctify—
the Warsaw Ghetto Memorial. Simple, fervid,
its grandeur and warmth reverberated to the height
and depth of my emotions, and I could not speak.

Your genius flashed into my finger-tips the last stand
against murderous Nazism in Warsaw stubbornly
continued by a few out of many famished and ragged
Jewish fighters that had given their all of blood,
sweat and endurance, and whose corpses lay
in dumbly accusing heaps round about. Shut off
from aid, betrayed, those surviving few yet kept faith
with themselves and humanity. In their gaunt faces,
charged with audacity, fire and straight-from-the-
shoulder sincerity, I sensed the Word of God
made flesh, an embodiment of superhuman qualities
that sleep in us for the most part.

Letter to Jo Davidson, Fall 1947

On the aftermath of World War II
───────────

𝒮adly, I anticipated when the late War ended,
that millions upon millions would be left without food,
shelter or medical care perhaps
for many years to come.
I cannot be happy here in America
with plenty to eat, warmth and wholesome diversion.
All I saw stabbed me to the soul last winter
when Polly and I visited the tragic world
of the blind—bombed London,
Paris still beautiful but desolate,
as full of bitter memories as London of bombings,
and everywhere evidence of a ruined civilization.

Letter to Frances [last name unknown],
in Nanking, China, undated [after WWII]

On the trial of the Scottsboro boys

*I*t is a bitter sorrow to me that millions of men
and women in this country are still exposed
to the cruelties of discrimination and prejudice.
My fingers tingle with indignation as I read
of the many lynchings in the South
and the dark sophistry with which Christians
seek to justify these barbarities. The judgment
by coming generations upon such travesties
of justice as the Scottsboro case
will be stern indeed.

Letter to James Weldon Johnson, January 31, 1935

On seeing Othello, *starring Paul Robeson*

*F*rom beginning to end we watched spellbound
the tragic passion and splendor of his acting,
and I was so overcome that I could not applaud.
Afterwards we went behind the scenes
to shake hands with Paul Robeson,
and I was as captivated by his great personality
off stage as in the drama. I told him I had read
Othello often and always with profound emotion,
but I had never found it so convincing,
or felt that any other actor had done full justice
to the big, simple, yet sublime African.

Letter to Clare Heineman, December 31, 1943

On racism in the United States

*T*he gathering at Danbury to urge justice to the negroes of Connecticut was impressive. . . . What I said at the Danbury meeting was only a sign of the unquenchable shame I feel over the situation of our colored people today. This revolt has never slumbered within me since I began to notice for myself how they are degraded, and with what cold-blooded deliberation the keys of knowledge, self-reliance and well paid employment are taken from them, so that they may not enter the gate of social competence. . . . The continued lynchings and other crimes against negroes, whether in New England or the South, and unspeakable political exponents of white supremacy, according to all recorded history, augur ill for America's future.

Letter to Nella Braddy, September 22, 1946

*P*ersonally I do not believe in a national agency
devoted only to the negro blind because in spirit and
principle I am against all segregation, and the blind
already have difficulties enough without being cramped
and harassed by social barriers.

*Letter to Mr. Auster, September 16, 1951, regarding the efforts
of the W. C. Handy Foundation for the Blind*

❦

On conflict in South Africa

I have some idea of the immense racial
and economic issues that are convulsing that land,
but, I have boundless faith in the potencies
of human nature, and I can look forward
to a society more excellent than any yet produced—
one that will turn its back upon race tyranny
and live according to the law
of brotherhood and justice.

Letter to Mathilde Davis, Cambridge, MA, ca. 1950

On the treatment of American Indians

*S*ince my childhood I have read all I could find
about the Indians, and my cheeks have burned
with shame at the terrible wrongs the white man
has done them and his violence
against peaceable disciples of the Great Spirit.
But I have learned much through wearing
the feathers of darkness and the moccasins of silence.
Like you I have in my heart the voice
of the free winds and faith strong
with the mountain's strength.
Standing among you I feel the Great Spirit near,
and I pray that your people may long carry
their message of life-giving wisdom
garnered from the sun, the waters
and the stars.

*Acceptance speech by Helen Keller to the Stony Indians
during the Annual Indian Week, Banff, Alberta, Canada,
July 21, 1939, and signed Helen Keller or "White Plume"*

On the United Nations

*F*riends took us to visit the United Nations twice last
autumn, and we listened to several deliberations—
one on Russia's latest proposal for atomic control
and another on whether Mr. Scott a Presbyterian
minister from South Africa should be permitted
to speak on the sufferings and wrongs inflicted upon
the natives. (I was delighted afterwards to learn that
he did speak in spite of strong British opposition.)
Of course the atmosphere of the United Nations is
frequently agitated and even menacing, but I still feel
that it is a hopeful, mighty instrument for world peace.

Letter to Claude F. [Dick] Dixon, 1950

~•~

On the development of nuclear weapons

I am terribly disappointed that more attention seems
to be given to the manufacture of nuclear weapons
than to progress in utilizing atomic discoveries
for the benefit of mankind.

*Letter to Waldo Mac Eagar
of the British Empire Society for the Blind, October 28, 1958*

On visiting the Empire State Building
————

*I*t was a thrilling experience to be whizzed
in a lift a quarter of a mile heavenward,
and to see New York spread out like a marvellous
tapestry beneath us. . . .
The little island of Manhattan, set like a jewel
in its nest of rainbow waters, stared up into my face,
and the solar system circled about my head!
Why, I thought, the sun and the stars are suburbs
of New York, and I never knew it! . . .
I was pleasantly surprised to find
the Empire State Building so poetical.

From every one except my blind friend I had received
an impression of sordid materialism—the piling up
of one steel honeycomb upon another with no real
purpose but to satisfy the American craving
for the superlative in everything. . . .
Well, I see in the Empire Building something else—
passionate skill, arduous and fearless idealism.
The tallest building is a victory of imagination.

Letter to Dr. John Finley, January 13, 1932

Triumph over Adversity

*T*he human being is born
with an incurable capacity
for making the best of things.

"O! Brave New World That Has Such People In't,"
Red Cross Magazine, *September, 1919*

A person who is severely impaired never knows
his hidden sources of strength
until he is treated like a normal human being
and encouraged to shape his own life.

Teacher, *1955*

*K*eep your face to the sunshine
and you cannot see the shadows.

Quoted in "Sundry Interviews," A Magazet, undated

━•━

*A*ny one can be happy, whatever one's lot may be,
if one has a reasonable, steadfast faith.
What really matters is the will to meet with courage
the difficulties of life.

Speech to fellow passengers
on the S.S. President Roosevelt, *October 1, 1930*

━•━

*W*e are not afflicted just because
we cannot see or hear. If we can love, work, play
and help others to be happy,
no matter how handicapped we may be,
we are capable of attaining
all precious things.

Letter to Doris and Elsie, two girls
whose mother was deaf-blind, undated

Triumph over Adversity

*T*he worst sorrows in life are not its losses
and misfortunes, but its fears.

"A New Thanksgiving and Prayer," undated

❧

*T*he chief handicap of the blind is not blindness,
but the attitude of seeing people towards them.

Speech for the American Foundation for the Blind,
Washington, DC, 1925

❧

*I*f we look resolutely, I will not say
at the bright side of things, but at things
as they really are, and avail ourselves of the blessings
we have, we shall realize the greatness of life,
and we shall find so much to do for others
that we shall have no time to dwell
on our own difficulties.

Letter to Rev. T. F. Glasson, Surrey, England, June 3, 1954

To Love This Life

*T*he true test of a character
is to face hard conditions
with the determination to make them better.

Letter to "Friends," March 30, 1921

❦

*W*hen the mind bends gladly to a task,
and the hand has to keep up with the eager spirit,
one feels in love with life,
in tune with the universe,
and misfortune loses its sting.

*Address to blinded WWI soldiers,
delivered at Evergreen Hospital, Baltimore, MD,
February 25, 1919.
Published in* Evergreen Review, *April 1920*

❦

*S*elf-pity is our worst enemy and if we yield to it,
we can never do anything wise in the world.

Quoted in Contemporary Quotations,
*compiled by James B. Simpson, Thomas Y. Crowell,
New York, 1964,
from news report of June 26, 1955*

*T*o keep on trying in spite of disappointment
and failure is the only way to keep
young and brave. Failures become victories
if they make us wise-hearted.

Speech at the Wright-Humason School,
New York City, Winter 1921

— • —

I believe that misfortunes are often the keys
which open doors of higher truth for us.

Letter to Mrs. William S. Burridge [Alice Hale],
October 27, 1953

— • —

*I*f we can't travel on the road we like,
let us not sit down by the way.
Let us look round about for the detour,
which may turn out to be more interesting than
the highway, and sometimes proves
the shortest way home.

Speech at the Wright-Humason School,
New York City, Winter 1921

*I*f we look at difficulties bravely,
they will present themselves to us
as opportunities.

*Speech to students at the Royal Normal College [England],
July 7, 1932*

❦

*W*e differ, blind and seeing, not in the nature
of our handicap, but in the spirit with which
we meet and conquer it.

*Speech delivered at the Kent Street Reformed Church,
Brooklyn, NY, 1927*

❦

*M*any of us delude ourselves with the thought
that if we could stand in the lot
of our more fortunate neighbor, we could live better,
happier and more useful lives. . . . It is my experience
that unless we can succeed in our present position,
we could not succeed in any other.

*Speech delivered at the Kent Street Reformed Church,
Brooklyn, NY, 1927*

*N*ever bend your head.
Always hold it high.
Look the world straight in the face.

Quoted in Contemporary Quotations,
compiled by James B. Simpson, Thomas Y. Crowell,
New York, 1964, from letter to a five-year-old blind child,
news report of May 31, 1955

---

*W*e all have limitations of one kind or another.
The only difference is in the way we meet them
with lifted head and smiling face.

Speech to students at the Royal Normal College [England],
July 7, 1932

---

*T*he problems of the blind are fundamentally
the same as the problems of every one else.
The difference is a matter of degree.
We, blind and seeing—we are parts of a great whole,
and we depend one upon another.

Speech to the Lions Club of Washington, DC,
October 19, 1925

*N*o one knows better than I
the bitter denials of life.
But I have made my limitations
tools of learning and true joy.

"Helen Keller at 80," interview by Ann Carnahan,
This Week Magazine, *June 19, 1960*

Selected Bibliography

BOOKS BY HELEN KELLER
Citations are from the original publications.

The Story of My Life, Grosset & Dunlap, New York, 1902

The World I Live In, The Century Company, New York, 1908

Out of the Dark: Essays, Letters and Addresses on Physical and Social Vision, Doubleday, Page & Co., New York, 1907

My Religion, Doubleday, Page & Co., Garden City, New York, 1927

We Bereaved, Leslie Fulenwider, Inc., New York, 1929

Midstream: My Later Life, Doubleday, Doran & Co., Garden City, New York, 1929

Let Us Have Faith, Doubleday, Doran & Co., Garden City, New York, 1940

My Key of Life (Optimism), Thomas Y. Crowell, New York, 1926; originally published in 1903 as *Optimism: An Essay*

Helen Keller's Journal, 1936–37, Doubleday, Doran & Co., Garden City, New York 1938

Teacher: Anne Sullivan Macy, Doubleday & Co., Garden City, New York 1955

The Open Door, Doubleday & Co., Garden City, New York 1957

Photo Credits

All photographs courtesy of the American Foundation for the Blind.

Cover

Helen Keller as a young woman, ca. 1903

Frontispiece

Helen Keller as a child, 1893

This Life

Portrait of Helen Keller with a dog, 1887 (Ira F. Collins)

The Senses

Helen Keller listening to the radio, ca. 1927 (A. Tennyson Beals)

Faith

Helen Keller writing longhand, date unknown

Happiness

Helen Keller on board a ship near the Orkney Islands, Scotland, ca. 1932

Friendship and Love

Portrait of Helen Keller and Anne Sullivan, Detroit, Michigan, 1918 (C. M. Hayes & Co.)

Life and Living

Helen Keller, Polly Thomson, and Herbert Haas at tea at Arcan Ridge in Westport, Connecticut, 1954 (still from the motion picture *Helen Keller in Her Story*)

Education

Helen Keller visiting the Lexington School for the Deaf, Jackson Heights, New York, February 23, 1947

Books and Literature

Helen Keller reading a braille book, ca. 1934
(A. Tennyson Beals)

Nature

Helen Keller in the garden of her home, Forest Hills, New York, ca. 1920

Women in Society

Helen Keller and Polly Thomson in Egypt, 1952

Human Nature

Helen Keller reading Anne Sullivan's lips with her fingers, Wrentham, Massachusetts, 1904

War and Peace

Helen Keller writing on a braillewriter at home in Westport, Connecticut (still from the motion picture *Helen Keller in Her Story*, 1954)

Changing the World

Helen Keller and an unknown boy, Durban, South Africa, 1950

People and Events

Helen Keller and Alexander Graham Bell conversing using the manual alphabet, Boston, 1902

Triumph over Adversity

Helen Keller receiving the Oscar awarded to *Helen Keller in Her Story* as best feature-length documentary of 1955, American Foundation for the Blind, New York, 1955

Endpiece

Helen Keller, ca. 1959